The Fourteen Wonders
and
Fourteen Treasures of
Ancient Britain

Eric L. Fitch

GREEN MAGIC

Green Magic
53 Brooks Road
Street
Somerset
BA16 0PP
England
www.greenmagicpublishing.com

Designed and typeset by Carrigboy, Wells, UK
www.carrigboy.co.uk

ISBN 978 1 915580 30 6

GREEN MAGIC

Contents

THE FOURTEEN WONDERS OF ANCIENT BRITAIN

CONTENTS

THE THIRTEEN TREASURES OF ANCIENT BRITAIN

(number variable, so I selected 14)

Introduction

This short book lists and describes *The 14 Wonders of Ancient Britain*, compiled by Nennius in the 9th century, and *The 13 Treasures of Ancient Britain* described in the 14th century. Many of the subject matters are concerned with Wales, south west England, and the "Old North" or Hen Ogledd, at the time when Celtic kingdoms existed from Cornwall and Wales up to southern Scotland. I have also added some wider material not directly connected, but still related to the subject matters, and a few of the illustrations feature items older than the period when the lists were written, but are relevant to their area.

I therefore present these lesser known aspects of Britain for the first time in such a format.

The Fourteen Wonders of Ancient Britain

COMPILED BY NENNIUS

INTRODUCTION

Nennius was a 9th-century monk based in what is now Powys in Wales, but that is about all we know of him. Apart from his religious responsibilities, he was the author of the *Annales Cambriae* (*The Welsh Annals*) and the *Historia Brittonum* (*A History of the Britons*). The latter work, dated to about 830, is the basis of this chapter, as it includes his *Fourteen Wonders of Britain*, most of which are in Wales or the west of England, chosen by Nennius as the most worthy of noting, and his work is significant as it contains the earliest reference to King Arthur.

At this time, long after the Romans had departed Britain, Wales was split into separate kingdoms. In 784, Offa's Dyke had been constructed, dividing the Saxons from the Welsh, so this is the background to Nennius's life. His *Historia Brittonum* aimed at tracing the Britons past the Romans and back to the Celts. It also records the mythical origins of the Picts and Scots, as well as dealing with characters such as the 5th-century Vortigern, King of the British at the time of the Anglo-Saxon invasions, who took refuge and died in North Wales.

Much of the "history" is not much more than stories and legends. Within the document appear the fourteen wonders, which describe ancient ruins, rivers, lakes, cairns and other landscape features which Nennius considered important enough to record in his plan to legitimise the origins of the British. The corpus places a mystical element to these sites, including the legends of King Arthur together with his twelve battles, even though Nennius was a Christian antiquary and monk and a disciple of Elvodugus, Bishop of Gwynedd. There are over 30 extant manuscripts of the *Historia* dating from the 10th century to the 13th, which also include accounts of St. Patrick, the six ages of the world, and 28 cities. I shall deal with the Wonders in alphabetical order.

Note: I have not translated Nennius myself, but have paraphrased and I have also added background information for each site, but have left out directions to each, which can be found on *The Wonders of Britain* website (see reference at Main Works Consulted).

Amr's Tomb

The village of Wormelow Tump, situated a few miles south of Hereford, used to be able to lay claim to a mound connected to King Arthur up till the end of the 19th century. In fact, it was said to have been the resting place of that legendary figure's son, Amr. Described by Nennius as Amr's Tomb, in recent centuries it has been known as the Wormelow Tump[1].

It is not well known that legend has it that King Arthur had three sons, apart from Mordred who died with Arthur, named Llacheu, Gwydre and Amr. Llacheu, who is mentioned in medieval Welsh poetry, notably in *The Black Book of Camarthen* and *The Dream of Rhonawby*, depicted a heroic character who was particularly important in early Arthurian literature and was killed prematurely before his father. Gwydre also died early, having been attacked and slaughtered by the giant boar Twrch Trwyth, as recorded in the tale of *Culhwch and Olwen*. None of

1 "Tump" derives from the Welsh *twm* meaning a tomb, and is widespread in the West Country denoting a small mound. The term "low" in the village's name comes from the Saxon *hlaw* meaning a burial mound. So, in effect, the place-name reads "Worm mound mound". As for the Worm element, this normally denotes a dragon, but there is no folktale to this effect attached to the village; perhaps its origin is in a Saxon personal name

the three sons seems to have been children born to Arthur's wife, Gwenhwyfar.

All that is known about Amr is that he was described as one of Arthur's four chamberlains, who guarded Arthur's household, another being Bedwyr's son, Amhren. Apparently, Arthur killed Amr himself and had the tomb constructed nearby, which was in the area called Archenfield[2], but why he did this grievous deed is not recorded. Nennius describes the latter's tomb as lying near a spring called Llygad Amr or Amr's Eye, now known as Gamber Head.

It is said that the Tump could not be measured more than once and achieve the same result. Sometimes it measured six feet in length, sometimes nine, twelve, and fifteen feet. Nennius says that he had tried this himself, and always failed. This folkloric feature is common with many prehistoric monuments, such as stone circles, where it is often said that one cannot count the number of stones in the circle more than once and come up with the same number each time.

Gamber Head spring is positioned precisely relative to the Tump, just as Nennius recorded. It is about a quarter of a mile from the Tump situated in a kind of bowl-shaped area and feeds Gamber Brook, a tributary of the River Wye. During hot spells, the Tump would have stood proud in the landscape, but in periods of rain, the trench surrounding the

---

2 Archenfield was the name given to southern and western Herefordshire by the Saxons, but it was originally part of the larger Welsh kingdom of Ergyng. The author of this book himself resides in the Archenfield locale.

mound would have filled up, and only the tip would be visible. I cannot find the origin of the word Gamber, but being the name of a brook, it is likely to be ancient. There is one possibility and that it is a corruption of a Welsh word, or even that it stems from the name Amr itself; Herefordshire has many Welsh place-names.

Sign pointing to a footpath leading to a bridge crossing the River Gamber. Pauline Eccles (Wikimedia Commons)

And now to the Tump's fate, for which I am indebted to the late Herefordshire author Mary Andere[3] for having done excellent work in the uncovering of the story behind the sad demise of the ancient monument in 1896, when it was destroyed in the process of widening a road. Andere was fortunate enough to be able to speak to an elderly gentleman who gave her details of a trial test which took place in 1885,

---

3 *Arthurian Links with Herefordshire*, by Mary Andere (1996).

but did not lead to an actual excavation at that time. To begin with, a two-pole section was taken at mid-height through the Tump, which revealed nothing. However, a vertical probe came up with a few bones and some ashes, but the latter were loose and not in an urn or other container, and it is not known where the bones ended up.

As for being flattened in 1896 without any thought of its historic and cultural importance just to widen a road, and on top of that not to investigate it archaeologically first, it was disgraceful even for the late 19th century[4]. It is surprising that no local antiquary stepped in to look over the monument as it was being demolished. And to lose the bones and ashes that were discovered in 1885 without preserving them at, for example, Hereford Museum, was outrageous. And in 1896, there should have been a watch on the demolition – who knows, the bones may have been the remains of Amr himself. Of course, modern dating methods only give the approximate date of the bones as well as where he originally came from, but at least it would have given us some indication as to his history.

---

4 This author used to live near Taplow in Buckinghamshire where an Anglo-Saxon burial mound is located, the finds of which were the most spectacular for that period before those at Sutton Hoo were discovered. The mound was excavated in 1883, which was carried out as a properly conducted archaeological dig, so there was no excuse for not doing the same thing at Wormelow Tump in 1885 and 1896.

The road near where the Tump was located, with the Tump Inn. Philip Halling (Wikimedia Commons)

The Tump survives in the village name, with the local pub The Tump Inn, as well as the local road Tump Lane. A sad end for one of Britain's Ancient Wonders.

WORK CONSULTED

Nennius: British History and The Welsh Annals, edited and translated by John Morris (1980).
This chapter was first published in issue #67 Mid-Summer 2020 of *Merry Meet* magazine.

Perhaps the mound looked like this Celtic burial mound at Gohmichele in Germany.

Manuel Heinemann (Wikimedia Commons)

The Appled Ash

This Wonder, ash trees bearing apples, could be found growing on a wooded hillside by the River Wye as it enters the Severn Estuary below Chepstow.

Of course, it is not possible for true apples to grow on an ash tree, but there is an explanation that fits the bill. The true service tree (to distinguish it from the wild service tree), whitty pear, or sorb tree (*Sorbus domestica*), whose leaves are similar to those of the mountain ash or rowan tree, brings forth fruit which resembles apples or pears called sorbs. These were harvested to make a drink like cider, a practice which still survives on parts of the Continent. They are unpleasant to eat straight after picking but, having been left awhile, they are edible and can be used to make jam. Apparently, the fruit tastes like dates and, in the past, were given to children as a form of sweet and sold at markets.

The tree can live up to 300–400 years and grow up

Illustration of the true service tree J.C. Loudon (1844) (Wikimedia Commons)

to 25m and may be indigenous to Britain or possibly introduced by the Romans, but it is now very rare, which has prompted plans to save the species. Sites where they can be found include Porthkerry Country Park in Glamorgan, various sites in Gloucestershire, and Shirehampton Nature Reserve near Bristol.

Natural monument sorb tree in Kronberg, Germany.
Heinz-Vale (Wikimedia Commons).

With climate change, it could be that lowland Britain will be more suitable for the tree, as it thrives on lime- and clay-based soils. They are hermaphrodite and are pollinated by insects, and the bark is made up of square cracked plates of a grey/brown colour. The trees' flowers are white and appear in close-knit clusters; however, they produce an unsavoury smell. The wood is hard, is suitable for polishing, and is a favourite for wood turning and making furniture.

Cabal's Cairn

CELTIC DOGS

Before I continue on the topic of King Arthur's dog, it is appropriate to have a brief say on dogs, or hounds, in the Celtic world.

The Celts bred large dogs for hunting, including wolfhounds, greyhounds and deerhounds, as well as being employed on the battlefield. In the *Mabinogion*, the First Branch begins with a hunt, where Pwyll, Prince of Dyfed, is chasing a stag with his pack of hounds. The Greek writer Strabo (c.64 BCE–c.24 CE) reported that British dogs were exported for their skill in hunting. They were also useful in protecting their masters from attacks by ferocious wild animals, such as bears and boars. On farms they acted as guard dogs, and smaller breeds were used in the control of vermin, especially rats, which had a taste for grain.

At a Romano-British temple near Nettleton Shrub in Wiltshire, the principal god was Apollo Cunomaglus, Apollo being a Roman hunting god and the latter Celtic name meaning Hound Lord. Many Celtic kings and heroes added hound to their names including Cunobelinus "Hound of Belinus" and Cu Chulainn "Culann's Hound". Dogs were also trained as healers, as the licking of their tongues over a wound was therapeutic. This practice was carried out at another Romano-British temple dedicated to the Celtic god Nodens at Lydney in Gloucestershire, where many images of dogs and the bronze statuette of a dog were discovered, the latter becoming the emblem of the Lydney Park Estate.

Illustration of a statuette of dog found at Lydney.
William Hiley Bathurst (1879) (Wikimedia Commons).

Celtic (Welsh) mythology had the notion of an underworld called Annwn, ruled over by Arawn, who possessed a pack of otherworldly dogs named the Cwn Annwn, or the Hounds of Annwn. With red ears and shining coats, they took part in the Wild Hunt led by Arawn, and were also known as ghost hounds, foretelling death and searching for corpses and the souls of humans.

CABAL, ARTHUR AND THE CAIRN

Cabal (Cafal, Caval) was the name of King Arthur's special dog, which was prominent in the hunt for the great boar Twrch Trwyth. This hunt occurs in the Welsh tale of *Culhwch and Olwen*, which features the earliest reference to Arthur[1]. During the hunt, Cabal does not kill the great boar, but does contribute to the death of the Ysgithyrwyn boar. Whilst the dog is chasing the animal, he leaves a footprint on a stone, which Arthur then places on top of a cairn made up of stones, coming to be known as Carn Cabal. Nennius adds that if anyone takes away the stone for a period of one day and night, the next morning it reappears on the cairn's top.

Lady Charlotte Guest (1812–1895) was the first to translate the *Mabinogion* from Welsh into English, published in parts from 1838 to 1845. She was also the first to recognise that the cairn was at the top of Carn Gafallt in the Elan Valley, about 13 miles northwest of Llandrindod Wells. So, sometime in the 1840s, she sent a gentleman to climb the mountain and report back to her what he found. The first observation was that there were a number of varying-sized cairns, some of which were at least 150 feet in circumference.

Cabals Cairn was eventually discovered, its appearance matching that recorded by Nennius, including the stone with the paw print on top, measuring about two feet long and nearly a foot

---

1 Arthur is not mentioned historically, leading historians and archaeologists to deny that he existed at all. However, my opinion is that there is no smoke without fire, and there must be a reason for his name to become so renowned, even though his existence cannot be proved and probably never will be. But aren't the Arthurian stories splendid!

wide, which could be lifted and carried off quite easily. On one side, an oval recess about four inches long, three inches wide and two inches deep could be seen, giving the impression of a dog's paw without too much imagination. However, it has been later pointed out that there are a number of cairns that have indented stones which could fit the bill.

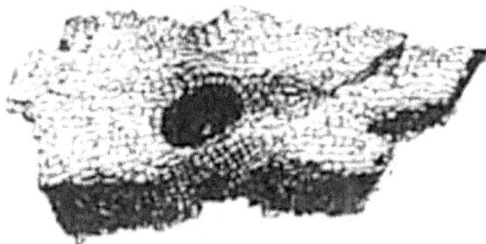

Sketch of stone with paw print, from Lady Guest's *Mabinogion*

As to Cabal's breed, it has been suggested that it was an Irish wolfhound, since the breed is ancient, very large and was well-known in Celtic times[2]. Cabal was also involved in stag hunts, and it was the custom that this hound was let off the leash last of all. It has also been claimed that the name Cabal is derived from the Latin word Caballus, which translates as horse or ass, which has caused some discussion on the subject. So here we must leave the topic for the scholars to sort out.

WORKS CONSULTED

Sacred Celtic Animals, by Marion Davies (1998).
Animals in Celtic Life and Myth, by Miranda Green (1992).

Crug Mawr Tomb

Translating from the Welsh, Crug Mawr means "great pile" – referring to a mountain with a grave on top. Nennius placed it in the country called Ceredigion, which was a minor mid-west Welsh kingdom up until about 1000 CE, becoming a county in 1282, corresponding to Cardiganshire, under the rule of Edward I. The area has been inhabited since prehistoric times, the Celts appearing on the scene after the Bronze Age. They constructed 170 hillforts, although some may have begun in the Bronze Age, and by the time the Romans arrived, the area was peopled by two Celtic tribes, the Ordovices and the Demetae.

Crug Mawr, thought to be the hill Banc-y Warren situated a couple of miles northeast of Cardigan, is 479 feet high, and it was the site of a Celtic hillfort and an artificial mound which is no longer extant, which was considered to have been the tomb. However, there is some debate whether Crug Mawr indicates the hill or the tumulus. Gerald of Wales (c.1146–1173), in his work, *Journey Through Wales* (1187), recorded that he observed the tumulus at the top of the hill. And local folklore stated that if anyone left a suit of armour there in the evening, by the following morning it would be found hacked to pieces.

Banc-y-Warren. Cered (Wikimedia Commons).

There was a tradition recorded by Peter Roberts in *The Cambrian Popular Antiquities* (1815) concerning Banc-y-Warren, which reads thus:

"... a powerful *cawr*, or *giant*, kept his post on this hill, who was endowed with the genius of the Ayeron vale. He had a lofty palace erected on the hill, and used occasionally to invite the neighbouring giants to a trial of strength on the top of it; at one of these meetings coits were proposed and introduced, and, after great efforts, the inhabitant of the spot won the day, by throwing his coit clear into the Irish shore, which ever after gave him the superiority over all other giants in Caredig land."

Nennius, as well as Gerald, pointed out another piece of local folklore, and that concerned measurements, as follows. If anyone, irrelevant of their height, stretches himself out adjacent to the grave, the latter is always reported to be found measured the same length of the person. Nennius also records that if any weary traveller bows three times near the grave, he will never, until the day he dies, find himself fatigued again, even though he goes to the edge of the universe.

Trig point on Crug Mawr (with Sugar Loaf in the distance).
James Ayres (Wikimedia Commons).

And finally, there seems to be no folklore as to who was buried under the mound, as in the case of Amr's Tump.

The Fiery Pool

This Wonder is probably the most well-known – the hot springs at Bath in Somerset. Nennius refers to the hot lake at the baths of Badon in the region of the Hwicce, a Saxon tribe. Enclosed by a stone and brick wall, men could bathe there at any time they pleased, choosing whichever type of bath suited them. If they wanted a hot or cold bath, both were available.

There are six hot springs to be found in the British Isles, but it is only at Bath that they can reach 45 degrees Centigrade, and every day over one million litres of mineral-rich water pour out of three springs, which emanate from the great depth of about 4,500 feet (about 1,350 metres). The hot water which emerges is due to the unique geological environment in the Bath area.

As to humans' use of the hot springs, this must have begun thousands of years ago, right back to the Mesolithic era, which commenced after the ice retreated about 12,000 years ago. When people started to settle down in this country, around 7,000 years ago (i.e. in the Neolithic and Bronze Age eras), it is hard to believe that they would not have made use of the springs, and almost certainly they would have treated them as sacred. The first people whom we can recognise utilising the springs were the Iron Age Celts, who dedicated them to their goddess, Sulis.

But now for the legendary story of the founder of Bath, Bladud, as written by Geoffrey of Monmouth. Bladud was the son of King Lud, who sent him to Athens for eleven years, where he contracted leprosy, and when he returned to Britain, he was locked away. However, he escaped and became a swineherd in a village not far from the future Bath, but he found that he had infected his pigs. One day, whilst meditating on what to do, he noticed that suddenly his pigs were running down the hill to which Bladud had driven them, and they began to wallow in the mud produced by the hot springs.

Bladud then set to cleaning the mud off the pigs, but he noticed that their skin had become free of the sores they had been suffering from. Observing this phenomenon, he had the idea that he would try washing himself with the springs' hot, muddy water, and he too was cured. Then he returned to his father's court and, when the time came, he became king and reigned for twenty years. During this time, Bladud built the city of Bath, or Caervaddon, and constructed the baths where the water healed the sick. Apparently, a number of ailments were healed by the warm springs, especially women's problems. He dedicated the springs to the goddess Sulis, and had a temple built containing fires that were kept burning day and night.

In addition, he encouraged learning, and arranged for scholars to be brought over from Greece, setting up a university. He was also a practitioner of the occult, and he designed a pair

King Bladud. Smalljim
(Wikimedia Commons)

Bladud flying over the
Temple of Apollo

of wings, with which he put on and flew over New Troy, or London, but plummeted fatally on top of the Temple of Apollo. The springs continued to be used into the Middle Ages, with lepers looking for a cure. Later writers expanded Bladud's pursuits to include astrology, astronomy, necromancy, therapy and shape-changing, and he was buried at Trinovantum, an early name for London. It was said that all this occurred in the 9th century BCE, with the plaque at Bath mentioning 863 for Bladud's presence there. His name derives from the Welsh words *blaidd* (wolf) and *iudd* (lord). He was succeeded by Leir, Shakespeare's King Lear.

Now we turn to the Romans. Arriving in Britain in 43 CE on the command of the Emperor Claudius,

Britain remained in the Roman Empire until 410 (i.e. for 367 years). With their architectural skills they built grand structures such as the Temple of Claudius in Colchester, which was flattened by Boudicca, Queen of the Iceni, in her revolt against Roman rule in 60 CE. Their buildings constructed at the springs would have been just as imposing. In the 3rd century, the Roman writer Solinus commented that they were luxurious, and the Roman temple built at the site with the goddess Minerva presiding over the springs housed the perpetual fire. The bath complex became famous throughout the Roman Empire, with the 2nd-century geographer Ptolemy referring to them as *Aquae Calidae*, or "The Hot Waters".

The dedication of the temple was to Sulis Minerva, which follows the Roman custom of merging a local god or goddess with one of their own deities. As well as their major gods, both the Celts and Romans believed in local gods, who needed to be placated, so there was no problem of the clashing of beliefs. Sulis was the local Celtic goddess, the meaning of whose name is not clear, and Minerva was the Roman goddess of wisdom. An intact carving of a gorgon's head was discovered at the site, but whether this represented Sulis is not known, perhaps it is a water or sun god. It is certainly Romano-Celtic and was positioned on the temple pediment surrounded by Roman imagery, a merging of the two cultures, a perfect representation to feature on the temple of Sulis Minerva.

Gorgon carving at Bath Roman baths.
Drow male (Wikimedia Commons).

Like many other sacred springs and pools and their connected deities, Sulis was probably a healing goddess, her name seeming to be linked to the sun, and her worship continued until about 350 CE. However, it has been confirmed that the spring water possesses medicinal minerals conducive to healing such disorders as gout and arthritis. So it is likely that Sulis was seen as a healing goddess[1]. One of Sulis's attributes was that of a goddess of vengeance. Excavations at the site produced 130 curses made from pewter and lead. These were inscriptions made onto the leaden sheets, asking Sulis to curse someone

---

1 Here I include a personal experience. When I was 14, I had warts on my hands which wouldn't go away. On holiday that year, my family visited the Roman baths and I bathed my hands in the spring waters, and in under two weeks my warts had disappeared. I now give belated thanks to Sulis.

who had done them wrong, and they were then cast into the waters. Often these were in revenge for clothes stolen whilst the devotee was in the baths, although others were connected to blood, fertility, sleep, and other disorders, and many of these curses were merciless.

Roman baths, Bath. Diego Delso. (Wikimedia Commons)

Of course, after the Romans left Britain, many of their buildings were briefly still being used, but eventually they fell into disrepair and their stonework was used for other buildings, such as churches, and, unfortunately, the bulk of Hadrian's Wall. However, there is still enough left to interest us in Britain, although we haven't got the large structural survivals as they have on the Continent.

I shall finish this section with the beginning of a poem entitled *The Ruin*, which was written in Anglo-Saxon probably in the 8th or 9th centuries, meditating on the remains of the Roman baths. It is translated into modern English prose:

"Wondrous is this masonry, shattered by the Fates. The fortifications have given way; the buildings raised by giants are crumbling. The roofs have collapsed; the towers are in ruins ... There is rime on the mortar. The walls are rent and broken away, and have fallen, undermined by age. The owners and builders are perished and gone, and have been held fast in the earth's embrace, the ruthless clutch of the grave, while a hundred generations of mankind have passed away. Red of hue and hoary with lichen this wall has outlasted kingdom after kingdom, standing unmoved by storms. The lofty arch has fallen ..."

–Trans N. Kershaw
(Cambridge University Press, 1922).

Bath hot spring. Engraving by W. Walker (1774).
(Wikimedia Commons)

WORKS CONSULTED

Mythology of the British Isles, by Geoffrey Ashe (1990).

Roman Bath Discovered, by Barry Cunliffe (2000).

The Waters of the Gap: The Mythology of Aquae Sulis, by Bob Stewart (1981).

"The Celtic Goddess as Healer" by Miranda Green in *The Concept of the Goddess*, edited by Sandra Billington and Miranda Green (2006).

RECOMMENDED FICTION

The Winged Man, by Moyra Caldecott (1993).

Blaedud the Birdman, by Vera Chapman (1978).

Fount Guur Helic

This Wonder is termed a spring by Nennius, situated in the territory named Cynllibiwg, which suggests a location between the rivers Wye and Severn, but there are arguments for other areas, with no agreement as to where the spring is actually located. The description indicates that it's a pool, Guur Helic appearing to be a personal name. Its depth is uniformly "up to the knees", and its measurements reveal it to be a square with sides of 20 feet, with high banks surrounding the pool, which implies that it had been fashioned by human hands. There are two singular features which stand out, and obviously Nennius thought them to be strange enough to receive the epithet "Wonder".

Firstly, the pool was full of fish, and men fished from each of the sides, with each side having a different species, leaving one wondering how such a comparatively small and shallow pool could support such a piscine variety and number. Secondly, there was no stream flowing into or out of the pool, which makes it all the more surprising that the pool contains fish at all. There are three main ways that fish can get into ponds with no stream connected:

(a) fish could be dropped accidentally into a pond by birds after they have caught them to eat;

Helicon or Minerva's Visit to the Muses. Joos de Momper the Younger (1564–1635).

(b) fish eggs could become attached to a bird's or other animal's body whilst it is drinking from a body of water containing fish, and passed on to another pond previously devoid of fish when the creature moves on, the eggs subsequently hatching;

(c) and/or deliberately by human action.

There is one other possibility that may explain the name Fount Guur Helic, and this comes from Greek mythology. The Mountain of Helicon in Boeotia is a place where the springs gave inspiration to poets when they drank from the waters. One of them was created by the hooves of the winged horse Pegasus, and the springs on Mount Helicon were sacred to the Greek goddesses the Muses, and the god Apollo. Is it possible that Helic = Helicon? Was the pool named after the springs at Mount Helicon? Latin, as well as Greek and Roman mythology, was known in Britain from the times of the Roman occupation, so is it possible that Helicon could have been a borrowed name from that period? I shall leave the subject for the reader to mull over.

The Levitating Altar

The story about this Wonder is based around the Welsh Saint Illtyd, who was born around the second half of the 5th century. Legend has it that he was the son of a prince in Brittany and rumoured to be a cousin of King Arthur, under whom he served for a period, and he was married to Trynihid, "a virtuous wife". However, he gave up his military activities, abandoned his wife, found God, and studied under St. Germanus in France, who taught him the traditional "seven sciences", i.e. Arithmetic, Astronomy, Geometry, Grammar, Logic, Music and Rhetoric.

After travelling around the Celtic areas of Brittany, Cornwall and Wales, where he set up churches, he ended up at what is now Llantwit Major in Glamorgan, where he founded a monastery. Although it is not certain where he died, Wales or Brittany, he passed away c.530, leaving behind him a church school which is reputed to be the earliest centre of learning in Britain. A few miles from Brecon, there is a cromlech called Ty Illtyd, based on the folklore that it was the saint's hermitage.

Now to Nennius's story of the Levitating Altar, which begins with St. Illtyd praying in a cave close to the sea. Whilst engaged in his religious devotions, his eyes suddenly caught sight of a ship heading his

Ty Illtyd. Henry Longueville Jones (1867).

way with two men and something he couldn't quite make out. As the ship drew closer, he could see that the other object was a body with an altar hovering over the face without any sign of how this was being held. When the ship reached the beach, Illtyd ran down to the shore to greet the men with welcoming words. The two men disembarked and told Illtyd that the body was of a holy man and that the altar was suspended over the body, which smelt sweetly, by the will of God.

Having told the saint the deceased's name, they urged him not to tell anyone else, so that no-one could swear by him. On his deathbed, the holy man had instructed them to take his body to Illtyd, where all three of them could bury him together. Having carried out the holy man's wishes, the two men departed and sailed away, leaving the grave and the altar still levitating over it. Illtyd then decided

St. Illtyd's Church, Llantwit Major.
Stevieb3945. (Wikimedia Commons).

to build a church around the grave and altar, and
many people who came to the church over the years
experienced miracles after visiting the sacred spot.

One day a local king paid a visit to the shrine to
test it, carrying a stick. He twisted the stick around
the altar, held the two ends with his hands and
tugged the altar towards him to see what would
happen. However, the altar did not move, and he
died within a month. Later on, another man decided
to peep under the altar, resulting in him going blind,
and he also expired in under a month.

Welsh legend has it that Illtyd was one of the
three knights of Camelot who minded the Holy Grail,
the others being St. Cadoc and Peredur. Cadoc was
the saint who converted Illtyd to the Christian faith,
after Illtyd's hunting companions were swallowed
up by the earth. Apparently, he was hunting in a

swamp close to Cadoc's monastery, and he was the only one who survived the calamity. It has been suggested that this story came about to ensure that Cadoc's monastery Llancarfan had precedence over Illtyd's. Students of Illtyd are said to have included St. Patrick, Taliesin, and St. David. There are other legends involving magical altars about Celtic saints arriving in Britain by sea on stone altars, millstones and barrels, and readers can follow these stories up if they so wish.

Llyn Lliwan

Described in a rather pell-mell manner by Nennius, this Wonder is some kind of whirlpool situated in an unidentified spot in the Welsh part of the River Wye, near to where the river flows into the River Severn. It appears that this feature, a tidal lake, occurs when the Severn Bore inundates the Severn River and the sea comes up to its estuary, thus forming a whirlpool. When the sea recedes from the Severn, everything that has been cast by sea into Llyn Lliwan is disgorged in a singular wave. Nennius adds that if anyone faces the wave, they will be sucked down into the water, but if they have their back to the wave, then all is alright and the water just ebbs naturally. It has been suggested that Whirls End in the Severn Estuary near Chepstow is the place where this natural event occurs, which does make sense, but there is no overall agreement on the subject.

Another version comes from Geoffrey of Monmouth's *History of the Kings of Britain*, published in about 1136. Here, he has King Arthur discussing the lake with another comrade. He describes a lake called Llyn Lliwan situated near the River Severn in Wales which, when the sea came up to it, gulped the seawater down as though it was a mountain, resulting in it flooding its banks. Like Nennius, he also told the tale that if any person stood facing the lake with spray wetting their clothes, they found it difficult to evade being sucked into the lake. But if they faced the other way, despite approaching close to the lake's edge, they were not affected at all.

The Severn Estuary and Portishead Pier.
ArticCynda (Wikimedia Commons)

Llyn Lliwan also turns up in the tale of *Culwch and Olwen* from the *Mabinogion*, where Arthur hunts the notorious enchanted boar Twrch Trwyth, boar-hunting being common in ancient Celtic times. This chase, which Arthur led with a large band of warriors, took place across southern Wales. The boar was once a prince named Twrch who had been magically transformed into the savage beast, whose bristles were poisonous, and who carried a comb, razor and a pair of scissors upon his head, between his ears[1]. The hunt began at Milford Haven and

---

1   There is much more to this story, so I recommend reading the *Mabinogion* for the full text.

continued through Pembrokeshire. It was on the way to Ewias that Arthur sent for reinforcements from Devon and Cornwall, and they met up at Llyn Lliwan, towards which the pursuers chased the boar, via the Severn Estuary and finally Cornwall, where the boar drowned off the coast.

And this seems to be the only other reference in early literature to Llyn Lliwan.

Tony Woodman's sculpture of Twrch Trwyth and piglets.
Nigel Davies (Wikimedia Commons)

Loch Lumonoy

In this loch were 60 inhabited islands; round its perimeter stood 60 rocks, and upon each was an eagle's nest, and 60 rivers flowed into it. However, only one river, the Leven, flowed out of the loch and eventually reached the sea, and, though not very long, only six miles, it was the second fastest-flowing river in Scotland.

The lake is assumed to be Loch Lomond, the largest lake in Great Britain by surface area, and is 22 and a half miles long and about five miles wide. In fact, it has 30-odd islands[1], including Inchmurrin, which is the largest freshwater island in the British Isles. It also contains a number of crannogs, artificial islands used for dwellings dating from the Iron Age, or perhaps earlier. The loch was formed by glaciers from the last Ice Age which gouged out a hollow into which water was trapped between 20,000 and 10,000 years ago.[2]

Geoffrey of Monmouth, in his *History of the Kings of Britain*, adds a couple more folkloric events about the loch. One is that the eagles which nest on the rocks surrounding the loch flocked together once a

---

1 There is a problem on what defines an island, but the number is not as many as 60.
2 This also applies to Loch Ness, which was formed around the same time, and which proves that the "Loch Ness Monster" could not be a relic dinosaur.

Loch Lomond by Horatio McCulloch (19th century)

year. On this occasion, they made a piercing screech, which was seen as a portent of some salient event which was to happen to the Scottish kingdom. The second concerns Arthur, who is said to have caused the death by starvation of thousands of Pictish and Scottish warriors who had landed on some of the islands to seek refuge in his aim to sweep the land of barbarians. This is another early tale involving the Once and Future King which predates the later chivalric legends.

The Returning Plank

This Wonder is another watery one, this time situated in the small village of Pwllmeyric in Monmouthshire. It translates as Meurig's Pool, referring to Meurig ap Tewdrig (Meurig son of Tewdrig). He was king of the ancient Welsh kingdoms of Glwysing and Gwent round about the 5th and 6th centuries. He joined with his father, Tewdrig, to defeat the encroaching Saxons at Pont y Saeson (Bridge of the Saxons), at which Tewdrig was killed. Meurig had his father buried in nearby Mathern, building an oratory there, and donating the neighbouring lands to the bishops of Llandaff.

Not much is known about Meurig, but his kingdom of Ergyng included Gwent, Glamorgan, Worcestershire and Herefordshire, thus ruling over the domain of the Celtic tribe, the Silures. He also assisted in the founding of the monasteries at Llancarfan and Llandaff, the latter being where he was buried. His eldest son, Athrwys ap Meurig (c.605–655), has been seen by some as the "real" King Arthur. St. Tewdric's Church, a Grade 1 listed building, is to be found in Mathern close to Meurig's Pool, which is not actually in Pwllmeyric itself. The local district being three miles or so southwest of Chepstow – it is not far from the Severn Estuary.

St. Tewdric. Martinevans123 (Wikimedia Commons)

Death of Tewdric
(Wikipedia)

Nennius states that there was a spring by the wall of Meurig's Pool, in the middle of which was a wooden plank, which men's feet could rest on whilst they carried out their ablutions. Nennius himself says that, apart from seeing this done firsthand, he had washed his own face and hands in the same manner, and that he confirmed that he had seen the plank itself.

When the sea causes flooding at times of the high tides, the River Severn bursts its banks, covering the whole of the shore, and the Severn Bore causes the spring to be filled, after which the waters recede into the sea, carrying the plank along with them. For three days the plank remains at sea upside down, and on the fourth day it is found in the spring once again.

Nennius also adds that once upon a time, a local peasant stole the plank from the spring and buried it, only for it to reappear in the spring four days later, with the peasant dying before the end of the month.

Old oak tree by the reen (drainage ditch) which flows from St. Tewdric's Well. Ruth Sharville (Wikimedia Commons).

What else can one say about this phenomenon? There is no natural explanation for it, so it remains another miraculous Wonder.

The Salt Fountains

Nennius describes this Wonder very briefly:

> "The Wonder consists of the salt springs that occur there, where the salt is extracted by boiling the spring water, which can be used to salt a variety of foods. They do not occur near the sea, but flow upwards from the earth."

These salt springs, three of them, can be identified as being at Droitwich Spa in Worcestershire, but first a little history and geology. The scientific definition of a spring is "a location where water emerges from the earth of its own accord". Salt, or brine, springs are common on the North American continent but uncommon in the UK. They form at the gravel and clay bases of valleys which become saturated with brine as it seeps down the valleys' sides. Salt mines and springs have been utilised by humans in Britain from Roman times and probably earlier. The Romans referred to both as *salinae*, giving us the word saline, but our word salt derives from the Anglo-Saxon *sealt*, both ultimately deriving from one Indo-European word[1].

Only fifteen miles from Droitwich are the springs and wells of the Malvern area of Worcestershire,

---

1 Indo-European is a hypothetical language from which many of the languages of Europe and India derive.

which has about 70 dotted about the hills; however, these produce mainly "pure" water, whereas the Droitwich springs are decidedly salty, as are those in Cheshire, such as Nantwich. Like these two towns, place-names with the suffix *wich* often indicate a settlement where some kind of early industrial, artisan-based or farm work took place. There is also a more specialised meaning of the word, and that is the existence of brine springs in the locality. It is of interest to point out that the Cheshire and Worcestershire salt workings were dealing with salt that was in ancient landlocked seas which dried up over time, leaving the salt deposits behind.

Droitwich Spa. Tanya Dedyukhina (Wikimedia Commons)

Each of the three Droitwich brine springs was named individually in medieval times, as Upwich, Middlewich and Netherwich, reflecting their positions in the town and also along the River Salwarpe, which begins near Bromsgrove and passes through Droitwich on its way to joining the River Severn. It has been suggested that the *Sal* in Salwarpe derives from salt or salinae, but the "official" derivation is that it's from sallow (yellowish-brown), referring to the river.

At Upwich, archaeological excavations in the 1970s and 1980s revealed that salt works had been in existence in the area from the Celtic Iron Age onwards. Evidence for this early period included hearths for the boiling of brine, timber-lined brine tanks, wells, and clay receptacles used for salt drying and transportation. Moving into the Roman period, finds included wooden barrels, ash, rope, timberwork and fragments of a winch, and the salt works continued into the Anglo-Saxon period and beyond[2].

The *Geography*, compiled by Claudius Ptolemy about the middle of the 2nd century CE, included the place-name Salinae, as did the *Ravenna Cosmography* drawn up in the early 8th century, recording the location as Salinis, both names referring to Droitwich. An early reference to the Droitwich salt works was in 716 in a grant made by King Ethelbald to Evesham Abbey of a salt pit[3]. The term *droit*, meaning a "right" in French, was attached to the town's name when it was given its charter by King John in 1215, the year he signed the Magna Carta.

2 English Heritage (https://historicengland.org.uk/listing/the-list/list-entry/1020256).
3 British Geological Survey website.

Droitwich Barge Canal was constructed in 1771 to aid the transport for the salt industry. In the 19th century, when the town became a spa location, its name finally became Droitwich Spa, and it is twinned with Bad Ems in Germany, another spa town.

Trahannon River

Thought to be the River Trannon, this Wonder concerns the mouth of the river, which is a chief tributary of the upper reaches of the River Severn. It joins the Severn near the village of Caersws in the county of Powys, formerly Montgomeryshire, the site of a Roman fort. In fact, the place-name Caersws derives from two Welsh words, *Caer* meaning "fort", but the meaning of the second element *sws* is uncertain; perhaps it refers to a Celtic leader, Queen Swswen, who is known to have fought a battle in the locality.

Site of the Roman fort near Caersws.
Rod Trevaskus (Wikimedia Commons)

Nennius tells us that a wave "like a mountain", presumably the Severn Bore, proceeds from the river mouth, floods the river banks and recedes in the same manner as a sea. There is some doubt, however, that the Severn Bore could reach the Trannon, but river courses do change over the centuries, so perhaps this accounts for the confusion. The river is important for brown trout, which spawn in it, and also for salmon.

River Trannon at Avon Cerist. Penny Mayes
(Wikimedia Commons)

And that, unfortunately again, is about all that can be said about this Wonder.

Two Kings of the Severn

The Severn Bore. Kate Lambert (Wikimedia Commons).

The River Severn Bore again. The two kings refer to two waves created by the Bore which have a skirmish with each other in the midst of the river. As Nennius describes the event in dramatic terms, I paraphrase him:

> "At the time of the Bore, the peaks of two waves are created individually and attack each other like belligerent rams. One rages against the other, and they clash each other in turn, and then one retires from his opponent, after which they repeat the battle at every tidal bore. This they have enacted from the creation of the world right up to present times."

There is a place where this phenomenon can be observed. This occurs in the eastern channel of the River Noose, when the first western wave rebounds off Hock Cliff and flows right into the following wave in the eastern channel. Hock Cliff is classed as a Site of Special Scientific Interest as it is a classic example of a Jurassic landscape, with its dense limestone and soft shale strata, and is an excellent place for fossil-hunting. At the site, fossils such as ammonites, belemnites, and crinoids can be found, and it has even been known to contain pieces of prehistoric marine animals, such as ichthyosaurus vertebra.

Hock Cliff. Peter Kwan (Wikimedia Commons).

This Wonder thus incorporates a natural phenomenon, and the site of contact with ancient life from millions of years ago.

The Wind Hole

The final Wonder from Nennius's list was situated in Gwent, but it has not been identified. He describes it as a crevice that blows out a wind that never ceases, even in the summer when there are usually fewer natural winds. This means that no-one can endure standing in front of the crevice, nor its depths, and the wind is a great wonder that blows from the earth.

It has been suggested that the location could be Wynd Cliff, which is a limestone cliff on the western bank of the River Wye in Monmouthshire, especially since it's close to some of the other Wonders. It does possess a number of large clefts which a wind could blow through, even though nowadays it seems that none have the wind element blowing from them. In general, wind emanating in caves and fissures can be due to the air pressure within changing all the time to equal the air pressure at the surface.

The origin of the name Wynd Cliff is said to have been derived from the two Welsh words *chwyth gwynt* meaning "the blowing of the wind", as opposed to the River Wye and "cliff", but others claim that Wynd refers to the winding bends the river makes as it flows on its way along this stretch. Wyndcliff Wood is a noted place as a fine example of gorge woodland. To climb to the summit of the cliff, where there is a viewpoint named the Eagle's Nest, there are 365 (not exactly!) steps, installed by the Duke of Beaufort in 1828. It has been claimed that nine counties can be viewed from the cliff top, as well as the two Severn bridges and the Severn Estuary.

Wynd Cliff face (365 Steps).
Nicholas Mutton (Wikimedia Commons)

Near Wyndcliff Wood on the hill top lies the site of a Roman villa, although all that can be seen now are cropmarks delineating where structures had been. However, recent metal detecting has turned up a piece of a bronze statue, which could indicate that the buildings were part of a temple complex. The whole was enclosed within a circular ditch, which was probably of Iron Age or Bronze Age date. Perhaps the temple ruins may once have looked something like the illustration below.

Roman temple at Benwell, Newcastle-upon-Tyne. Engraving by John Collingwood Bruce (1885). (Wikimedia Commons)

The cliff is popular with climbers, but until the late 1960s the site was hidden by a blanket of ivy, which was eventually removed, enabling climbers to practise their hobby. Apparently, the climbers pronounce "Wynd" to rhyme with "pinned", whereas the local inhabitants rhyme it with "find", which is probably the time-worn traditional pronunciation.

And now another point of interest. At the bottom of the 365 steps there used to stand a thatched dwelling named Moss Cottage, whose windows were made of stained glass surrounded by Gothic ornamentation. Unfortunately, it was demolished sometime in the last century. In the days when coaches would take tourists who were on return journeys from Chepstow to Tintern, they allowed one hour to climb the steps and back, as well as take tea at the cottage. Here they would imbibe their infusion whilst seated at a table made from the

View of the Wye Valley from the Eagle's Nest. Nicholas
Mutton (Wikimedia Commons)

Moss Cottage in the 19th century. The National Library of
Wales (Wikimedia Commons)

wood of a certain walnut tree that once flourished in the ditch at Chepstow Castle.

And finally, for those interested in geology, Wyndcliff is made of Lower Dolomite rock, sitting above the less firm Lower Limestone Shale, which has collapsed over the millennia and has reached the river. The area is mainly covered with ancient woodland which was once coppiced, and is made up of ash, beech, hazel, lime, whitebeam and yew.

I leave the reader with this marvellous 19th century illustrated view of the scenery surrounding the last Wonder described.

The Fourteen Treasures of Ancient Britain

COMPILED FROM LATE MEDIEVAL WELSH MANUSCRIPTS

INTRODUCTION

Even though they are always referred to as Thirteen Treasures, the actual number can vary depending on how they are counted, but whatever the number, they are still referred to as Thirteen. For instance, the Crock and Dish of Rhygenydd Ysgolhaig can be regarded as two treasures or one, and sometimes Eluned's Stone and Ring are included, and sometimes not. I shall therefore deal with fourteen, to match the number of Wonders. The accounts of the Treasures derive from late medieval Welsh legendary texts, and most are placed in the previously Celtic-speaking regions of northern England and southern Scotland. As with the Wonders, I shall deal with them in alphabetical order.

The reader will also come across the Welsh story *Culhwch and Olwen* in a number of the Treasures, so rather than keep on reiterating elements of the tale, I shall summarise it here.

After the death of his mother, Culhwch's father, King Cilydd, remarries, but Culhwch's stepmother wishes him to marry his stepsister, which he is emphatically against. His stepmother, taking umbrage at Culhwch's attitude, places a curse on him, which means that the only woman he can marry is the beautiful daughter of the giant Ysbaddaden named Olwen. Rumour had it that the giant's eyelids were so weighty that the only way he could open them was to support them with forks or spears. Although Culhwch has never set eyes on Olwen, he grows more and more infatuated with the thought of her.

To assist his son in his quest to find Olwen, Cilydd advises him that he would not be able to find her unless his cousin King Arthur is brought in to help out, after which Culhwch immediately sets out to consult him. Reaching Arthur in his Cornish court at Celliwig, the renowned king consents to assist him by sending out a search party to find Olwen, to no avail after looking for her for one year. Arthur then gathers together his most worthy warriors, including Cai, Bedwyr and Gwalchmei (later known as Sirs Kay, Bedivere and Gawain), to search again. The band eventually comes across a shepherd whose wife is Culhwch's sister, but she tries to dissuade him from finding Olwen, as every man who has done so before disappears. Undaunted, Culhwch is intent on finding Olwen, so much so that the shepherd's wife let it be known that Olwen comes to their house and washes her hair there every Saturday.

One Saturday, Culhwch eventually meets up with Olwen and is overcome with her beauty, and straightaway falls in love with her, and she with him. However, she tells him that they cannot be wed unless her father consents to the pairing. Ysbaddaden, with the knowledge that he is destined to die when Olwen is wed, will not permit the marriage unless Culhwch completes a number of tasks which, on the face of it, seem to be impossible, especially one which involves cutting her father's hair and shaving his beard, which eventually he performs as the last task. Ysbaddaden then dies, and the couple get married.

Legend has it that the Thirteen Treasures are kept by Merlin in his Glass Tower, with the wizard asleep alongside them, on Bardsey Island off the coast of North Wales.

The Cauldron of Dyrnwch the Giant

The features of this Treasure are that:

(a) if a man of courage deposits a slab of meat into the cauldron, it will immediately boil without the cauldron being heated; and,

(b) if a cowardly man does the same thing, then the meat will remain raw forevermore, however hot the cauldron may be.

The magic cauldron figures not uncommonly in both Welsh and Irish mythology – two features especially being of note. Firstly, there is the cauldron connected to battles, where warriors who have been killed are thrown into it, re-emerging alive again, but without the power of speech. Such a cauldron was owned by Bran the Blessed, the Welsh god of rebirth.

The other is the cauldron of plenty, which produces a never-ending supply of food, with the Irish god Daghdha possessing a huge example of such a vessel. Irish kingship also involved the use of a cauldron, where the new King of Ulster had to bathe in it, whilst at the same time eating the flesh and broth of a white mare to which he had ritually "wedded". The 12th-century writer Gerald of Wales reported that the kingship ritual also involved the mock mating of the king with the horse beforehand.

Many cauldrons have been immersed in lakes or bogs in the Celtic countries of Scotland, Wales and Ireland, which are deemed to be ritual deposits, dating back to around the 8th century BCE. The famous Gundestrup Cauldron, found in Denmark in a peat bog in 1891, is dated to the 1st century BCE and is highly decorated with scenes including an antlered god surrounded by a number of animals, three ram-horned snakes, mythical beasts, a sacred hunt chasing three bulls, a goddess in a chariot accompanied by more otherworldly animals, three trumpeters carrying a Celtic carnyx, and much more. One scene in particular shows a giant hurling a warrior upside down into a cauldron, perhaps representing a dead warrior as mentioned above.

Celtic cauldron. Boldwin (Wikimedia Commons)

In medieval Welsh writings, there are a number of other texts featuring cauldrons, such as those mentioned in the *Tale of Taliesin*. Arthur himself in *Culhwch & Olwen* attempts to gain possession of Dyrnwch's cauldron via the Irish King Odgar in vain. However, Bedwyr grabs hold of the cauldron and hands it over to one of Arthur's servants, who carries it off loaded onto his back. After a successful fight with a band of Irish men, Arthur and his retinue manage to board Arthur's ship, Prydwen, landing back in Britain with the cauldron and other booty.

The Gundustrup Cauldron. Nationalmuseet, Copenhagen
(Wikimedia Commons)

It has been suggested that the Holy Grail was developed from the Celtic cauldron, but if so, it must have been by oral folklore tradition, and this cannot be proved. In any case, the first French romances from the 12th century mentioning the Holy Grail describe it variously as a stone, dish or cup, suggesting that it was an invention detached from any earlier Celtic object. However, there was a development over the centuries from the utilitarian use of the family cauldron into a symbol of spiritual rebirth. This theme is contained in the *Tale of Taliesin*, where the enchantress Ceridwen possesses a cauldron of poetic inspiration. In the tale, Ceridwen's son Gwion is transformed via the cauldron from a nondescript boy into the renowned poet Taliesin.

The word "cauldron" derives via Norman French from the Latin *caldarium*, meaning a "hot bath". The archaeological record shows that cauldrons were in use in the Bronze Age, which preceded the Celtic Iron Age. The most well-known cauldron is that used by the three witches in Shakespeare's *Macbeth*:

> "Double, double toil and trouble;
> Fire burn and caldron bubble.
> Cool it with a baboon's blood,
> Then the charm is firm and good."

To round this subject off and bring us up to date, the Olympic Flame that burns while the Olympic Games proceed rests in a cauldron. Of course, the original Olympic Games ran from 776 BCE until 393 CE.

The Chariot of Morgan Mwynfawr

This vehicle will transport anyone wherever they want in double-quick time.

Morgan Mynfawr (618–710 CE), which translates as Morgan the Wealthy, was the grandson of Meurig ap Tewdrig (see also Wonder 10). He ruled over Gwent and Glywysing, the latter being a sub-Roman petty kingdom up until the early medieval period. He possessed land in Gwent, Glamorgan and Gower, thus ruling over much of southeast Wales, his forename Morgan eventually morphing into the modern Glamorgan. Probably his kingdom extended to include a section of Erging, which also covered a part of Herefordshire.

The *Book of Llandaff* contains charters relating to grants he bestowed to the Church of Llandaff, and an entry concerning ecclesiastical measures against him by Oudoceus, the third Bishop of Llandaff in the 6th or 7th centuries, who accused Morgan of killing his uncle, Ffriog. He is mentioned in the Welsh Triads, which consist of history, folklore and mythology grouped together in threes for rhetorical emphasis. Here he is referred to as one of three Red Ravagers, or destroyers, of Britain, the other two being Lleu Skilful Hand and Rhun son of Beli, and all three were termed one of the Noble Triads. Tradition has it that Arthur himself was the figure of Red Ravager, greater than the other three. Wherever one of the three walked, no grass or plants would grow in their tracks for one year, but in the case of Arthur, this would last for seven years. However, on the other hand, Morgan was also supposed to be a cousin of King Arthur as well as one of his knights.

Turning to chariots, the earliest chariots date from about 2000 BCE in the Eurasian Steppes. They became the favourite war vehicle of the Celts. However, they fell out of use in Gaul by the end of the 3rd century BCE, but carried on being used by the Britons up until Roman rule, with the image of Boudicca riding against the occupiers. 21 chariot burials from the Celtic Iron Age have been discovered in Britain, dating from around 300 BCE up until the Roman invasion – although this is not as many as they have found in Gaul. Most of those excavated in England have been discovered in the East Riding of Yorkshire and belong to the Parisii tribe, which came over from Gaul. The first, and so far the only, chariot burial in Wales was discovered by a metal detectorist in Pembrokeshire in 2018, an area which was inhabited by the Demetae tribe, the origin of the name Dyfed.

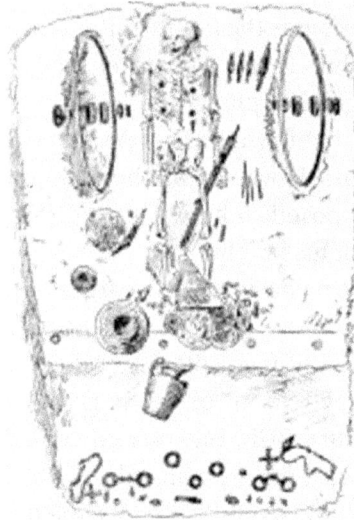

Plan of a Gaulish chariot burial from *An Introduction to the Study of Prehistoric Art*, by Ernest Albert Parkin (1915). (Wikimedia Commons)

Artefacts found in chariot burials include, obviously, the remains of chariots, but also horse accoutrements and sometimes horses themselves, weapons, metalwork, brooches, and pottery. The individuals who were buried thus were either chieftains or those of high status, and the person in the Yorkshire Wetwang Slack burial was a woman, which is unique in Britain. Women in Celtic times, as far as can be gleaned, had more influence over whom they married and as recipients of inheritances, than in the contemporary Classical civilisations.

After Boudicca's husband Prasutagus died, she was to share his inheritance with the Romans, but they reneged on the will's clauses and demanded the whole inheritance, which Boudicca objected to. The Romans then whipped her violently and raped her two daughters, which led to the Boudiccan revolt in 61 CE, where she, with her Iceni tribe, sacked Colchester, St. Albans and London before eventually being defeated, whereupon it is likely she committed suicide. There is a well-known statue of Boudicca in her chariot on the Thames Embankment in London (see below).

Boudicca in her chariot. (Wikimedia Commons)

The Roman geographer Pomponius Mela, writing about 43 CE, said that the British Celts used chariots drawn by two horses called covinni, whose axles were equipped with scythes, but this last fact has been doubted by scholars. None of the chariots discovered in Celtic graves had such scythes. However, a scythed chariot is featured in the Irish tale, *The Cattle Raid of Cooley*.

Interestingly, Da Vinci produced an illustration of a scythed chariot, shown below.

The Chessboard of Gwenddoleu ap Ceidio

This chessboard was made of gold and silver squares, with the 32 chessmen crafted from crystal and embellished with the same two precious metals. It was also magical in that the pieces played by Gwenddoleu would make his moves automatically by themselves.

Chess in the form we know it today can be dated to the 15th century CE, although there were former versions which had not developed this far. The famous Lewis Chessmen, discovered on the Isle of Lewis in the Outer Hebrides in 1831, date back to the 12th century, but despite consisting of 78 pieces, they do not make up a complete set, although it seems that they could have come from five separate sets. Most of the pieces were carved from walrus ivory, and it has been suggested that stylistically they were made in Trondheim in Norway between the late 8th century and the late 10th century CE. The characters of the chessmen are very similar to those in use today, so the game was well on its way to being what is played in modern days.

Pieces of the Lewis Chessmen. (Wikimedia Commons)

Now to Gwenddoleu ap Ceidio, who was an historical figure, a descendent of Coel Hen, whose name evolved into Old King Cole. His rule covered southwest Scotland and northwest England, known as the Celtic "Old North", in the 6th century CE. In the Welsh Triads, he is referred to as one of a trio of what were called Bull Protectors of Britain, and he possessed two birds yoked together by a golden yoke. These birds, probably ravens, were said to devour daily two dead bodies for dinner and another two for their supper. The name of the tiny village of Carwinley, located just within the border of England, is said to derive from Caer Gwenddoleu, or Gwenddoleu's Fortress, and it is now in the parish of Arthuret (Arfderydd).

Merlin was said to have been Gwenddoleu's adviser, but the ruler does not feature in Arthurian literature otherwise, and he died at the Battle of Arfderydd in 573. In Geoffrey of Monmouth's *Life of Merlin*, Gwenddoleu's death drove the wizard mad grieving for the king, leading him to flee into the Caledonian Forest, but other than this, there is nothing else known for certain about him[1].

---

1 See also Treasure 6.

The Coat of Padarn Beisrudd

This coat has the property that if a well-bred man donned it, then it would adapt itself to the person's size, whereas if a peasant tried it on, the coat would not fit his body.

Padarn Beisrudd translates as "Paternus of the red robe", and he was born in the early 4th century CE. His epithet probably derived from the fact that as a ruler in a Roman province, he was entitled to wear the Roman purple (in fact red), as in the Roman Empire this colour was reserved for the officials and the elite only. He ruled over the northern kingdom of Manaw Gododdin, which was probably centred on the modern town of Clachmannan, and he commanded a troop of Votadini foedorati. The latter were tribes who fought for the Romans on the Empire borders, in return for receiving land to settle on, as well as being paid.

The illustration below gives you some idea of a Celtic British warrior, complete with cloak.

The red dye required to colour clothing was extracted from several related species of shellfish,

---

* Out of interest, St. Padarn was born in Brittany and came to Wales, later founding a settlement in Cornwall, where he died in about 560.

Gallo-Roman statue of a Gaul warrior wearing Roman clothes and weapons. Found: circa 1850 in Vachéres, Alpes-de-Haute-Provence, France. (Wikimedia Commons).

specifically sea-snails in the Muricidae family. Thousands upon thousands of these sea creatures were necessary to make enough dye, a process which was extremely laborious to produce, involving boiling the unfortunate creatures for up to a week. The shellfish were to be found near the Phoenician coast of the eastern Mediterranean, nowadays known as Lebanon, and the dye acquired the name Tyrian purple, as this refers to the town of Phoenician Tyre. It was also known as Phoenician red, royal purple and imperial purple, and the dye was so indelible that even sunlight would not cause it to fade, and this led to its becoming exceedingly valuable.

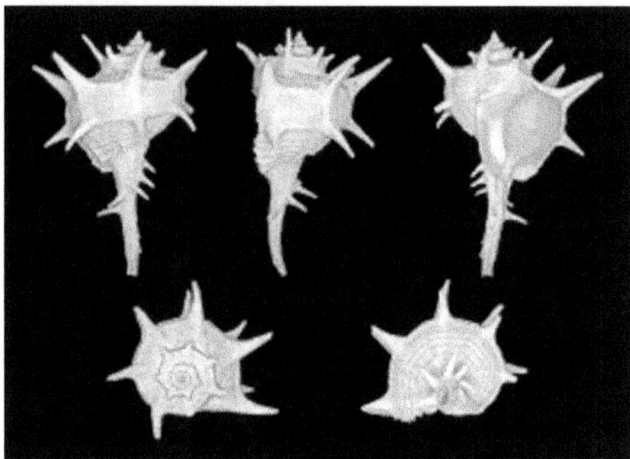

Purple dye murex shell. H. Zell (Wikimedia Commons)

Two further points. One of the Treasures' list claimed that the coat also ensured that anyone who wore it would never come to any harm. Secondly, another Padarn, the 6th-century St. Padarn, wore a similar coat which Arthur coveted, but he would not give it up. Arthur then went off fuming, only to come back with his feet flattening the ground as he walked. Padarn then requested God to let the earth engulf Arthur, who was buried up to his neck until he admitted his guilt and pleaded for forgiveness. It may well be that this singular tale originated from Padarn Beisrudd's red coat.

The Crock and Dish of Rhygenydd Ysgolhaig

The magical attribute concerning these two items is that whatever a person wished to eat would miraculously appear in both.

The name Rhygenydd Ysgolhaig, "The Scholar", does not appear anywhere else other than in the lists of the Thirteen Treasures. As monasteries were the repository of brewing and wine-making as well as learning after the Romans left Britain, it is appropriate that he would possess such a miraculous vessel.

It is not known how monasticism arrived in Britain, but Christianity had been established during the Roman occupation. Celtic Christianity did not have the inflexible structure of the Roman Church and interpreted the scriptures as they saw them. However, the Celtic Church held sway in Britain until the Synod of Whitby in 664 decided that the Roman way was the correct interpretation of the Bible. After the departure of the Romans, monasteries became more numerous, with a great expansion in the 6th and 7th centuries.

The British Celts were great meat eaters, devouring deer, boar, bear and beaver, as well as

---

* A crock is an earthenware pot or a vat.

Celtic cooking pot, original print in the 1901 book by J.M. Edwards, '*Y Mabinogion*', Wrexham (1901). (Wikimedia Commons)

fish such as salmon and trout. Domestic animals, including pigs, sheep and chickens, provided meat and eggs. Vegetables included turnips, parsnips, spinach, onions and carrots, and favoured seasoning herbs were parsley, garlic, fennel, sage and rosemary. Emmer grain was used to make bread and porridge, and also bees were kept for honey, and nuts and berries were widely available. Their meals were swilled down with wine and mead – which is where we have to leave this Treasure.

Dyrnwyn, the Sword of Rhydderch Hael

This magical sword bursts into flame along the length of the blade the instant a well-bred man draws it, but it does not burn him.

Unlike the last Treasure, this one has more background to be explored, and to begin with, Rhydderch Hael himself must be considered.

According to the Welsh Triads, Rhydderch Hael was deemed to be one of the Three Generous Men of Britain, the other two being Mordaf and Nudd, but Arthur was said to be more generous than all three. His name, Rhydderch, translates as "reddish brown", and Hael is Welsh for "generous". Rhydderch derives from Germanic origins, as in the English and German Roderick, and the Latin Rodarchus. He was the ruler of the British kingdom Alt Clut, situated in Hen Ogledd or "The Old North", from about 580 to 614. Being under the patronage of St. Kentigern lets us know that he was a Christian, and he was married to Gwenddydd, the sister of Myrddin or Merlin[1].

Joining up with various rulers from the Old North, he fought against the invading Angles from Bernicia at Ynys Metcaut, or Lindisfarne, and the only other military campaign in which he was involved was a

---

1   See also Treasure 3.

raid on the kingdom of Strathclyde along with Aedan mac Gabrain, the King of Dal Riata. Rhydderch eventually died of old age, without any progeny. Local legend has it that the Clochoderick Rocking Stone in Renfrewshire marks the place of his burial, which also served as a meeting place for the local Druids.

Clochoderick Logan (Rocking) Stone. Rosser1954 Roger Griffith (Wikimedia Commons)

There are two possessions attributed to Rhydderch, namely his horse called *Rudlwit*, or "Dun-Grey", and his magical sword *Dyrnwyn*, translating as "White Hilt", denoting the sword's handle made from bone. Named swords were a feature of Celtic culture, the best-known being King Arthur's Excalibur, or in Welsh *Caledfwich*, the latter translating as "Hard Cleft". In mythology, the smith gods, such as Hephaestus (Greek), Vulcan (Roman), and

Wayland (Germanic), were revered, as the work they performed in changing base metal into wonderful pieces such as swords, other weapons and jewellery was considered to be magical.

The fact that the forging process involved the use of fire links in with the *Dyrnwyn's* legendary bursting into flame. The Celtic smith god was Gofannon (Divine Smith) in Welsh mythology, who is featured in the *Mabinogion,* and his work also involved the cleansing of farmers' ploughshares. In the tale of *Culhwch and Olwen,* one of Culhwch's undertakings was to arrange for the plough owned by his brother Amaethon to be sharpened by Gofannon. Like Hephaestus, who was one of the twelve gods of Olympus, he was a major deity who, when invited to the court of any chieftain, had the privilege of having the first drink or toast.

Celtic sword and scabbard c.60 BCE
(Wikimedia Commons)

In Celtic Gaul, variations of his name appear as Cobannus, Gobannus and Gobanos, and in Ireland as Goibhniu. The latter made the weapons which allowed the Tuatha de Danann (the fifth wave of immigrants to Ireland, acknowledged as gods) to defeat the Fomors (a race of semi-human monsters).

Statue of Vulcan in Birmingham, Alabama. Guiseppe Moretti (1904). (Wikimedia Commons)

Unfortunately, there is no extant history of *Dyrnwyn*. So, apart from what is described above, nothing further can be said about this particular sword.

WORKS CONSULTED

Blacksmith Gods: Myths, Magicians and Folklore, by Pete Jennings (2014).
Celtic Myth & Legend, by Mike Dixon-Kennedy (1996).
Everyman's Dictionary of Non-Classical Mythology, compiled by Egerton Sykes (Revised edition, 1962).

Eluned's Stone and Ring

A magical gemstone affixed to the ring which, when someone obscures it with their hand, renders that person invisible. To make themselves reappear, they simply have to remove their hand from covering the stone.

This ring and its stone appear in the tale of *Owain, or the Lady of the Fountain*, which makes its appearance in the *Red Book of Hergest* and the *White Book of Rhydderch*. The figure of Owain is based on the 6th-century figure Owain mab Urien, son of King Urien of the kingdom of Rheged. As to Eluned, she is the handmaid of Laudine, the Lady of the Fountain; her Welsh name translating as "image" or "idol", and in Arthurian legend, she is described as intelligent and courteous.

A précised extract of the tale tells of Owain, a Knight of the Round Table, riding into the Castle of Landuc[1], belonging to Laudine, Lady of the Fountain, Owain having beaten her husband in combat earlier. He is suddenly trapped by the portcullis, but looking beyond into the castle interior he catches sight of a maiden with golden tresses and clothed in a garment

---

1 The Castle of Landuc is situated near Broceliande in Brittany, which has strong Arthurian associations. Here can be found a megalithic monument named Merlin's Tomb, which I have visited, being a bit disappointed as it is badly preserved and not that impressive.

of yellow. She then notices Owain and walks to the gate and opens it for him and his horse to enter, and it turns out that she is Eluned. She helps Owain by imparting to him a magic ring containing a precious stone, which provides him with protection and the option of making him invisible. Eluned then invites him to a chamber where they eat and drink, after which Owain falls asleep. In the middle of the night, he wakes and hears a cry which, Eluned informs him, means that Laudine's husband has died.

Later, Owain marries Laudine, having been advised to do so by Eludet. However, over a period, he neglects his knightly deeds and is absent from King Arthur's court, and they part. But later, he realises that he had not been a good husband, and, again with the assistance of Eluned, he gets back together with his wife.

A silver Roman finger ring found in Britain dating from 100-300 CE. The panel contains the inscription TOT, an abbreviation for the Celtic god, Toutatis Lincolnshire County Council (Wikimedia Commons)

INVISIBILITY AND RINGS

The two subjects mentioned above have ancient origins, and both of them are often connected, which I shall briefly relate.

An early account of invisibility concerns the Ring of Gyges, which occurs in Plato's *Republic,* where Gyges, a shepherd, steals a golden ring from a body he finds in a tomb inside a cave. After examining it, he discovers that when he twiddles with it, he can make himself invisible. He then proceeds to the royal court and, invisible, he seduces the queen and, with her assistance, murders the king, thereby taking the throne for himself as King of Lydia. This tale is obviously a forerunner of that described above, as folklore subject matter spreads across lands and times. Another example is the Helm of Hades, the god of the underworld, which Perseus also used in the killing of the Gorgon Medusa.

As to rings, perhaps the most well-known are the Rings of Power in Tolkien's *Lord of the Rings* trilogy; the One Ring, which Smeagol found, had the power of invisibility, and Tolkien was very influenced by the Celtic and Norse mythologies, especially the latter. Here, magical rings were owned by Odin and those of the Niflungs, a race of subterranean dwarfs, and in Norse mythology they were powerful symbols. Odin's golden ring was called Draupnir, which had the property of multiplying itself, whilst Thor's Domhring was a ring of doom. Those held by the Viking heroes gave them power and riches, although they could bring misfortune if perverted by greed. Turning again to rings, the composer Wagner's *Ring Cycle*, consisting of four operas collectively called *Der Ring des Nibelungen*, deals with a gold ring which gives its owner superhuman power and supernatural vigour.

In the second branch of the *Mabinogion*, the character Caswallawn uses a cloak of invisibility in order to commit murder. And another similar case is that of *Doctor Faustus* in Christopher Marlowe's play, where, after making a pact with the Devil, he gains magical powers, including that of invisibility, which leads to him playing tricks, such as boxing the ears of the Pope.

To wind up this section on rings and invisibility, I cannot omit H.G. Wells' 1897 novel, *The Invisible Man*, which, although it does not involve a ring, does highlight the dangers that invisibility, and science in general, could bring about when tampering with.

Claude Raines as *The Invisible Man* in the 1933 film directed by James Whale. Ryan McCleary (Wikimedia Commons).

The Halter of Clydno Eiddyn

This magical horse's halter was affixed to the foot of Clydno Eiddyn's bed, and any horse he desired would miraculously appear in the halter.

Clydno Eiddyn was a historical figure from the 6th century who ruled the kingdom of Eiddyn, which was roughly the area surrounding modern-day Edinburgh – thus giving the city its name. He later became a character in Welsh tradition, but little else of importance about Clydno survives, apart from one or two minor battles.

Horses' halters are important in controlling the animals, consisting of a strap fitting behind the ears and around the muzzle, which is used to tether the horse when stationary so that it cannot run away, and also to enable the owner to lead the horse to where it is needed. Horses were highly esteemed in both the Celtic and Anglo-Saxon worlds, and it is probably for this reason that horse meat is not generally eaten in Britain and Ireland to this day.

White horses have been portrayed on Britain's chalk hillsides for many centuries, although quite a few are of 17th- or 18th-century origin. However, the strange looking White Horse of Uffington in Berkshire has been examined scientifically and

Celtic horse helmet. Royal Scottish Museum, Edinburgh.
Kim Traynor (Wikimedia Commons)

found to date from the Bronze Age or the Celtic Iron Age, sometime between 1000 and 100 BCE. Such hill figures need to be scoured regularly as they soon disappear, but the antiquity of the Uffington example leads to the conclusion that it has been scoured continually for the amazing period of around 3,000 years.

The horses used by the British Celts were comparatively small to what we are used to, perhaps similar to Exmoor ponies. They were not kept for heavy work (that was usually done by oxen), but instead used for pulling chariots, ceremonial purposes, in war, hunting, and as baggage carriers.

Uffington White Horse. Public Domain (Wikimedia Commons)

Horses were considered animals of high status, especially in times of war, and head-hunting Celtic warriors would come away from battle with the enemy's heads tied to horses' necks, which the warriors used as votive offerings to their gods.

Sometimes, horses were buried alongside their owners, an example being a chariot burial excavated in northeast England, where the (probable) chieftain's body was interred, but also his horse team as well. Ritual activity involving horses was also carried out. For instance, at the Iron Age hillfort at Danebury in Hampshire, it was discovered that the skull of a horse had been deliberately placed in a pit used for storing grain – such a deposit not being found elsewhere in the archaeological record.

One tribe in Scotland called themselves the Epidii (People of the Horse), whose territory originated on the island of Islay, which spread to the islands of Jura and Arran, as well as Kintyre on the west coast of Scotland, their name deriving from the Celtic *epos* meaning "horse". It is likely that the horse was a totem animal of the tribe, which reinforces the importance of the animal to the Celts. *Epos* is similar to the Latin for horse, *equus* – both the Celtic languages and Latin having a common Indo-European origin.

Archaeology has shown that horse-worship in Britain existed at least from Celtic times or even back to the Bronze Age, when they were totem animals used in rituals concerning kingship – which leads us to horses as sacred animals linked to a god, or more often to a goddess, which we turn to now.

The reverence for the horse is reflected in the worship of a horse goddess named Epona, who was essentially a deity of the Continental Gauls, but there is also a little evidence that she was worshipped in Britain as well. A very popular deity, her name is obviously related to the Celtic word for horse, and her worship extended from Britain to Bulgaria, and was favoured by soldiers, especially in Romano-Britain. Equally important was the reverence of the goddess by ordinary people, her image often giving the impression of a mother goddess, as well as that of fertility and healing. She also was seen as a deity officiating over birth and death. Gaulish depictions of her sometimes show her accompanied by a raven, the bird of death, and many figurines feature Epona's image riding side-saddle or feeding horses.

Other Celtic horse deities include Echdae (horse god), and from Welsh tradition, Rhiannon, who has been seen by some scholars as linked to Epona. Rhiannon was recorded as giving birth to twins, one a baby boy, and the other a colt, which revealed her nature reflecting humans' reasoning aspect, as well as that of animal instinct.

Relief of Epona and horses from Germany. Wetterau Museum in Friedberg. Haselburg-Müller (Wikimedia Commons)

The Celts also worshipped other horse gods, in particular associated with the sun, evidenced by Celtic coins bearing the images of sun symbols, such as a chariot wheel, with these depictions emphasising the fertility, intelligence and speed of horses.

Celtic gold stater of the Iceni, with the depiction of a horse
15 BCE–20 CE Numisantica (Wikimedia Commons)

The Celts were experts in horsemanship in all of its aspects, which is reflected in their religion, legends and folklore, which are too complex to go into here, but if the reader wishes to find out more, then I can recommend the books detailed below.

WORKS CONSULTED

Animals in Celtic Life and Myth, by Miranda Green (1992).
Sacred Celtic Animals, by Marion Davies (1998).
Epona: Hidden Goddess of the Celts, by P.D. MacKenzie Cook (2016).
The Mabinogion (various editions).

RECOMMENDED READING (FICTION)

The Mark of the Horse Lord, by Rosemary Sutcliff (first published 1965).

The Hamper of Gwyddno Garanhir

If food enough for one man is placed in the hamper which is then closed, when opened, sustenance for a hundred men would miraculously be found in it.

Legend has it that Gwyddno Garanhir was the ruler of the sunken land, Cantre'r Gwaelod, off Cardigan Bay. His main stronghold was Caer Wyddno, situated northwest of what is now Aberystwyth, and his realm was fortified from being drowned by the sea by floodgates which had to be closed before the onslaught of high tide. Unfortunately, one day, the man who minded the gates became drunk and neglected to shut them, so that the sea poured in and flooded the land. Over the centuries, there have been tales of sightings of structures beneath Gwyddno's realm, which have probably been derived from surmising that natural submarine ridges were actually the vestiges of protective sea walls. However, local tradition held that there was a tract of land in his kingdom that was landlocked where he could hold sway.

His epithet Garanhir translates as "Long Shanks" or "Crane Legs" – *garan* means "crane" and *hir* "long". Cranes' appearance, with their long legs, the colours of their plumage, their elaborate mating "dances" and the formations they make whilst in flight, have led to them having links with Annwn, the Celtic underworld. They were considered to be birds to avoid, as they were looked upon to be creatures of ill omen – although, in Ireland, the crane was associated with poets and literary secrets, and in the Classical world it was linked with the god Apollo, the crane dance seen as a joyous celebration of life. Cranes became extinct in Britain, the last being shot in 1908 on Anglesey, but they have been reintroduced in recent years. Gwyddno's epithet suggests that he was a tall, lanky man.

Photo of a crowned crane. PanWoyteczek
(Wikimedia Commons)

There have been a number of suggestions as to who Gwyddno was, but the favourite is Gwyddno ap Clydno, the 6th-century King of Meirionydd, who was the father of Elffin ap Gwyddno, the foster father of the famed Welsh poet Taliesin. Gwyddno appears in *The Story of Taliesin*, where he is described as owning a coracle or basket in his fish weir, which was renowned for producing ten pounds of salmon every Nos Galan Gaeaf, or Hallowe'en. It was on this eve that spirits of the dead were abroad, and people avoided crossroads, stiles and churchyards. Taliesin lived in the 6th century, and some of his poems were included in *The Book of Taliesin*, compiled in the 14th century.

Taliesin Stone, Llanfair Caereinion, Powys, Wales. Set into the churchyard wall of the parish church. (Wikimedia Commons)

There is another manuscript which includes Gwyddno titled *The Dialogue of Gwyn ap Nudd and Gwyddno Garanhir*, where the scene is the aftermath of battles with the task of dealing with the dead. Here, Gwyn offers Gwyddno protection, as Gwyn announces that he was present at various battles where a number of British kings perished. Gwyn was the king of the fairy folk and King of Annwm, the Celtic underworld, and in later tradition he became a leader of the Wild Hunt. But here we end Gwyddno's appearances in medieval Welsh literature, and we turn to his hamper.

Gwyddno's hamper was probably a wicker basket, which the ancient Britons were skilled at weaving, and it is conceivable that Gwyddno's was a specially woven one. In the tale of *Culhwch and Olwen*, Culhwch is told by his stepmother that he would not marry until he met Olwen, daughter of the giant Ysbaddaden. However, the giant gave Culhwch 40 impossible tasks that he had to fulfil before he could wed Olwen, which included obtaining Gwyddno's hamper. So, with the assistance of Arthur and his knights, Culhwch set out to tackle the tasks[1].

RECOMMENDED READING (FICTION)

Silver on the Tree, by Susan Cooper (1977). This is the fifth and final volume of Cooper's *The Dark is Rising* sequence, which features Gwyddno as King of the Lost Lands.

---

1 See Introduction for a fuller account.

The Horn of Bran Galed

This magical drinking horn will be filled with whatever drink the imbiber prefers.

The word *galed* translates literally as "hard", but his name is usually referred to as "Bran the Niggardly". The name Bran, of course, is better-known as the character "Bran the Blessed", who was the giant Lord of Harlech in Welsh mythology, whose head was cut off and buried near what became the Tower of London, facing towards France.

A contemporary of Rhydderch[1], his birthplace and life remain unknown, but his parents were recorded as being Dyfnwal (father) and Ymellyn (mother). In a list of warriors from the north whose souls were taken by Gwyn ap Nudd to the underworld after dying in battle, he was mentioned alongside Gwenddolau[2]. He died at a battle fought at Cynwyd, at an unidentified location, and his inclusion in the list indicates that he was a person of some note, perhaps a northern king.

A 16th-century text refers to Myrddin asking the noblemen and kings of Britain for their treasures. They agreed to this on one condition, which was that he acquire Bran's horn, believing this would be an impossible undertaking. Nevertheless, Myrddin

---

1 See Treasure 6.
2 See Treasure 3.

managed to take possession of the horn, in addition to the other treasures as well, which he then transferred to his Glass House, where they would be stored for time immemorial.

Drinking horns were symbolic of abundance in Celtic times, much like the Classical cornucopia, and they were a major feature of feasts in the Celtic world. As well as preparing cauldrons full of ale and mead, the participants were able to refill their horns as they wanted. Ale had to be consumed within a short space of time, as it deteriorated quite quickly. Mead, on the other hand, was produced from honey extracted from wild bees' hives, and this was the only sweetener around for the prehistoric societies of Europe to use. This made the substance very precious, and so mead was drunk mainly by the higher echelons of society.

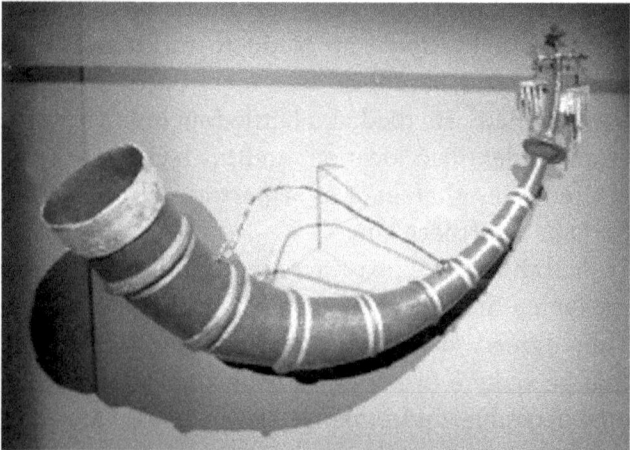

Celtic drinking horn c.530 BCE. Found in Hochdorf, Germany (Historic Museum of Bern). (Wikimedia Commons)

An 1893 depiction of the *Norse goddess Sif* holding a drinking horn. (Wikipedia)

Horns were often carved with intricate designs, some were banded with metal, and some were even made of gold. The everyday horns made of animal horns do not survive in the archaeological record, although the metal fittings of ceremonial examples have been found, as the illustration above shows.

In the 1820s, in a peat bog at Torss Moss in Scottish Kirkcudbrightshire, two drinking horn mounts were discovered, dating from about 200 BCE, both made of thin bronze and terminating in depictions of duck heads, a motif popular in mainland Britain. They were probably votive offerings made to the gods[3].

A description of the use of horns from the now-extinct giant cattle called the aurochs was recorded by Julius Caesar in his *Gallic War*. Here, he notes that the drinking horns used by the Gauls vary in size, shape and character from the Roman versions, their rims were fitted with silver, and they were often much in demand. Over the centuries, of course, horns eventually developed into the sophisticated instruments which we have today, such as the French horn and the cor anglais, with other related examples like the trumpet, trombone, cornet, tuba and euphonium. But they all originated with cattle!

WORKS CONSULTED

Everyday Life of the Pagan Celts, by Anne Ross (1970).

---

3 These were connected with the horse helmet described in Treasure 8. Opinion varies as to whether they were originally drinking horns.

The Knife of Llawfrodedd Farchog

This knife would serve enough meat for 24 men to eat at table.

Llawfrodedd Farchog (knight or horseman) was a Welsh hero who was a member of Arthur's court, who appears in two tales from the *Mabinogion* – *The Dream of Rhonabwy* and the tale of *Culhwch and Olwen*, both of which include long lists of men, including Llawfrodedd, belonging to Arthur's entourage. That is about all that can be said of him.

Knives of some sort have been used by humans from time immemorial, so it is not surprising that they crop up in Celtic tales, specifically with respect to feasting. Meat needed to be cut, the favourite animal being the pig or boar, which has been confirmed by bones found in archaeological excavations. When warriors were engaged in a feast, fighting took place between two opponents at a time to see who was the bravest, the winner being awarded the choicest cut of pork. This custom was recorded by Classical writers such as the polymath writer Posidonius, who wrote about the tradition in Gaul, where the fighting could end in fatality.

Pork was also featured in the Celtic Otherworld, where feasts also took place, many stories involving the eating of the meat. Such Otherworld pigs were consumed, followed by their returning to life the next day. Boars were associated with gods, with one in particular worshipped in Britain, named Vitiris, who was favoured by young Celtic warriors, and was also popular amongst Roman soldiers. In Celtic mythology and legends, pigs and boars feature many times, and in Welsh tales, boars could speak to humans and were associated with the underworld, and both porcine animals were shape-shifters.

A distinctive pig was that mentioned in the Welsh tale of *Lleu Llaw Gyffes*, where a swineherd informs the magician Gwydion that a sow of his leaves his abode every morning, but each time he loses track of where she ends up, so he asks Gwydion for his help in this matter. The magician manages to follow her tracks and comes across her filling her stomach in a valley named Nantlleu, beneath an oak tree where Lleu Llaw Gyffes is perching in the form of an eagle, in a tale which is too long to retell here[1]. Ultimately, the sow leads Gwydion back to Lleu, where he then changes him back into the form of a man.

In the ancient world, the wild boar was a creature to be revered. Perhaps the most well-known was the Erymanthian Boar – capturing alive this fierce creature was the fourth labour of Heracles. In Celtic mythology, the boar named Twrch Trwyth was an animal to be feared[2]. The Roman writer Strabo went so far as to say that the boar in the Celtic world was

---

1 For the whole story, see Miranda Aldhouse-Green below, pp.135–7.
2 See Wonder 8 for more of its story.

so fearsome that even a wolf would not go anywhere near one.

Replica of a carnyx with its boar's head found in Scotland in 1816. dun_deagh (National Museum of Scotland). (Wikimedia Commons)

The power of the boar led to Celtic warriors bearing its likeness on their shields and helmets, and when they went into battle, they were accompanied by trumpeters who carried carnyces, or war trumpets, whose sound openings were fashioned into the shape of boars' heads. These instruments were made of bronze and were very long, and when carried into battle their sound openings were held high above the warriors. They made such an awesome and terrifying sound, which filled the enemy with dread and caused them to be confused and fall into disorder.

There are many mentions of the boar in relation to food and also in supernatural accounts, with stories indicating that its meat was not only favoured by humans but also by the gods. It was considered

A modern reenactor demonstrating the playing of a carnyx.
(Wikimedia Commons)

to be the best creature to hunt, and it was admired for its strength, its fearless defence of itself, and its fervent appetite for acorns, the oak being a sacred tree to the Celts. There was a tribe on the Orkneys who took their name from the wild boar, the Orci, or Boar People. It can therefore be said that the boar was probably the most significant and sacred animal in Celtic society.

Wild boar with hunting dog on a Roman relief, 3rd century
CE. Römisch-Germanisches Museum in Cologne.
(Wikimedia Commons)

WORKS CONSULTED

Everyday Life of the Pagan Celts, by Anne Ross (1970).
The Celtic Myths: A Guide to the Ancient Gods and Legends,
by Miranda Aldhouse-Green (2015).
Animals in Celtic Life and Myth, by Miranda Green (1992).
Sacred Celtic Animals, by Marion Davies (1998).

The Mantle of Arthur in Cornwall

Whoever was covered by this cloak became invisible, but the wearer could observe everybody else.

First, a note about King Arthur. The earliest records of him occur in Welsh legend, where the tales in which he features are a far cry from the later tales of the Knights of the Round Table, Excalibur, Camelot, and the Holy Grail. The Welsh accounts have several stories featuring Arthur, in particular *Culhwch and Olwen*[1] and *Peredur*. He is portrayed as a figure involved in tales which contain Christian imagery as well as Pagan myth.

In *Culhwch and Olwen*, he appears as ruler of Brittany, Normandy and France, as well as King of Britain, but he is not shown as being central to the main story, nor is there much detail about him. In fact, in *Rhonabwy's Dream* he does not seem to be heroic at all. He is soaked by a horse splashing whilst crossing a ford, but it is one of his men who beats the animal. After this encounter, he plays chess with Owein, one of Arthur's chief warriors, who ignores his leader's requests and who acts as though he is of equal rank with Arthur. These events show not a

---

1 See Introduction and Wonder 8.

great leader, but rather a somewhat weak character, totally at odds with the later Arthur's romances at Camelot.

As for Cornwall, there are many connections with Arthur, with legends associating him with:

(i)   Tintagel (where he was born);

(ii) Bossiney Mound (under which lies the Round Table);

(iii) Slaughter Bridge (where the Battle of Camlann took place and Arthur died);

(iv) Killibury Castle (one of the places where Arthur held court);

(v)   Castle-an-Dinas (a hillfort where Arthur's Hunting Lodge is sited);

(vi) St. Endellion (the saint said to be Arthur's goddaughter);

(vii) Dozmary Pool (where Sir Bedivere threw Excalibur, as requested by the dying Arthur);

(viii) King Arthur's Hall on Bodmin Moor (a monument with unknown date or purpose);

(ix) Trethevy Quoit (a megalithic tomb also known as Arthur's Quoit);

(x)   Three of the Scilly Isles, named Great Arthur, Middle Arthur and Little Arthur; and,

(xi) Sites linked to Merlin, Tristan & Isolde, and King Mark[2].

Further to these Cornish places, there is one other Arthurian connection with Cornwall, which involves

---

2   I leave the reader to discover these.

the chough, a bird of the crow family. Once quite common in the county, it became extinct there in the 1970s; however, there are now a number of breeding pairs again. The bird's significance in Cornish history and folklore has always been prominent, and its image is featured on the Cornish coat of arms. In the Cornish language, now being revived, its name is "palores".

Chough. (Wikimedia Commons).

In Cornish folklore, it is believed that the spirit of King Arthur inhabits the Cornish chough, and there is a tale that demonstrates this. In 1113, a party of nine canons from Brittany came to England to raise funds for the restoration of their cathedral at Laon. Upon reaching Cornwall, they were shown the local sites associated with Arthur. However, when they reached Bodmin, a furious argument broke out between one of the clerics and a local man on whether Arthur still lived, the latter claiming that Arthur lived on in the form of a chough, the quarrel ending in a brawl in the local church. In addition, it appeared that at that time the Bretons disagreed about Arthur with their neighbours, the French, as well.

In 1924, the Federation of Old Cornwall Societies was formed, and adopted the bird as its emblem, as well as a Cornish motto which translates as "He is not dead, King Arthur". The annual Cornish Gorsedd, the meeting of the bards of Cornwall, has a custom of singing a song titled in English "He shall come again". Its last two lines are translated as:

> "Where shall we find King Arthur? His place is sought in vain.
> Yet dead he is not, but alive, and he shall come again!"

Coat of Arms of the Duchy of Cornwall. (Houmout means courage). Sodacan (Wikimedia Commons)

Turning now to Arthur's mantle. In *Rhonabwy's Dream*, Arthur was presented with the cloak which was made of damasked brocaded silk, featuring a reddish-gold apple on all four corners, and which went by the name of Gwen, meaning "blessed" or "white". The mantle also had the property that if anyone tried to dye it in any other colour, this would be rejected, leaving its original colour untouched. It was here that its quality of making its wearer invisible was made known[3].

In *Culhwch and Olwen*, Arthur refuses to give Culhwch his mantle, his sword Caledfwich, his dagger Carwennan, his spear Rhongomyniad, his shield Wyncebgwrthucher, and his ship Prydwen. Strangely, in the case of his mantle, there is no mention of Arthur ever using it, nor is there any explanation as to why it is associated specifically with Cornwall. So we have to leave things at that.

WORKS CONSULTED

King Arthur Country in Cornwall, by Brenda Duxbury and Michael Williams, introduction by Colin Wilson (1979).

The Folklore of Cornwall, by Tony Deane and Tony Shaw (1975).

The Lore of the Land: A Guide to England's Legends, by Jennifer Westwood and Jacqueline Simpson (2005).

---

3 For more on invisibility, see Treasure 7.

The Mantle of Tegau Eurfron

Her mantle, when worn by another woman, would reveal if she had committed adultery or lost her virginity before marriage and by choice, in which case it would only reach down to her waist, but if she was faithful, then it would reach to the ground.

Tegau Eurfron was the wife of Caradoc, who was Arthur's chief elder residing at Celliwig in Cornwall. Tegau Eurfron (*teg*=pretty, *eurfron*=golden breast) was one of the Three Chaste Wives at the court of Arthur (the other two being Enid and Dyfr), and their happy marriage led to them being called one of the Three Surpassing Bonds of Love in the British Isles. Her father was Nudd Hael (Hael the Generous), the 6th-century King of Selcovia, named after the Selgovae tribe.

How Tegau gained her epithet of Golden Breast has two versions. One says that she lost one of her breasts in battle, which was replaced with one fashioned from gold. Another states that she rescued Caradoc from a poisonous serpent, but in the process the snake bit her on the breast, which had to be cut off and replaced in gold so that her life could be saved. Thence she became a heroine of Welsh legend, owning not only the magical mantle but also two other treasures – a carving knife and a cup.

Although men generally ruled the roost in Celtic society, women were allowed some rights and freedoms, such as personal activity and protection enshrined in law, which was unusual in the ancient world. A woman could not be forced into a marriage if she did not want to, but marriages arranged for political purposes were not uncommon in the case of noble women. Having married, she could get divorced if she wished, and could remarry without being looked down upon. In addition, a woman was permitted to own property in her own right, and could take on a legal dispute without having to refer to her husband.

Turning to religion, the priestly caste were the Druids, an order which allowed women to enter, but little is known about them as they did not commit their teachings to the written word. Perhaps they are best known for an account by the Roman writer Pliny the Elder (c.24–79 CE), including that in Britain, the Druids enacted other magical rituals which involved a great deal of ceremony. The Druidesses often acted as seers or prophetesses, such as the Irish Druidess named Fedelm in the Irish epic *The Tain*. They could also be involved in business affairs and diplomacy without the consent of their husbands, including acting as intermediaries and judges in matters of a military or political nature, which extended to tribal assemblies.

The Druidess. Alexandre Cabanel (1823–1890).
(Wikimedia Commons).

There are other accounts by Classical authors who recorded the existence of a settlement of nine virgin priestesses named the Gallisenae on an island called Sena off the Brittany coast, which was forbidden to men. Their activities included healing, as councillors, and maintaining an oracle which was consulted by travellers. They were even said to foment the waves and winds by their ritual incantations, and were also said to have been shape-shifters, transforming themselves into any creature they wished.

Boudicca wearing a mantle. (John Opie - Easy Art, 18c.)
(Public Domain, Wikimedia Commons).

But the most well-known band of Druidesses were those who were massacred, along with their male counterparts and warriors, on Anglesey (Latin *Mona*) by the Romans in 60 CE. Tacitus describes them as carrying flaming torches and dressed in black clothing, with their hair sweeping behind them, whilst they ran amok amongst their Celtic comrades. The Romans achieved their goal, that is, the undoing of the Druid caste, although there were probably some who held the teachings in secret.

As warriors, Celtic women were just as capable as the men, although in a different way. They would wave their weapons in the air, dance around vigorously, pulling faces and shrieking, which must have been a startling sight to the enemy, especially when accompanied by the frightening cacophony of the carnyces (see Treasure 10). The most famous female warrior was, of course, Boudicca. After her husband's death, the Romans did not take kindly to a queen of a tribe and had her flogged and her two daughters repeatedly raped. She then led her tribe of the Iceni against the Romans and, at first, was successful in fighting and massacring them, as well as laying waste to Camulodunum (Colchester), London (Londinium), and St. Albans (Verulamium). However, she ultimately failed, and it is assumed that she took her own life rather than face a Roman humiliation and execution.

The Whetstone of Tudwal Tudglyd

This miraculous whetstone had the power to discover if a man was brave or a coward. When a sword was honed on the whetstone by a courageous individual, it would wound his enemy, with the injury always proving to be mortal. However, if the man was cowardly, after sharpening his sword, it would always fail to draw blood.

Tudwal Tudglyd, whose name translates as "People's Defender", ruled the kingdom of Alt Clut, an alternative name for Strathclyde, in the mid-6th century CE, and was the father of Rhydderch Hael[1]. There is not much known about him, only that he was blinded by St. Ninian for not accepting Christianity, but was later healed by the saint after converting to the new faith.

Sharpening weapons dates back to the Neolithic age, when stone axes were required to be kept sharp. There is a fine example of this near Avebury stone circle called The Polissoir or Polisher, the grooves made in the process being very clear. When metal weapons came on the scene – first bronze, and then iron – swords needed to be kept sharpened, bringing in the tool called the whetstone.

---

1 See Treasure 10.

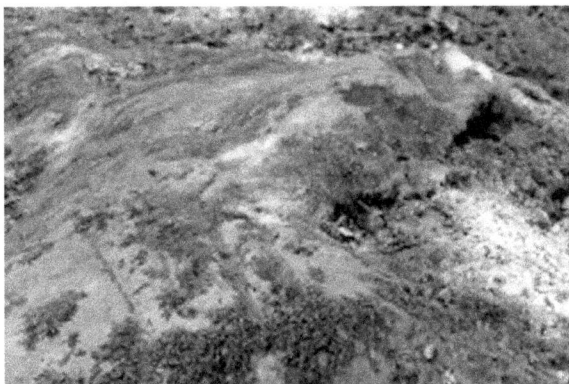

Neolithic polissoir, Sauvageon, France (grooves at left).
Robin Chubret (Wikimedia Commons)

Made from hard gritstone or sandstone, whetstones used by warriors in the so-called Dark Ages were seen as magical implements, and those that were first-rate were highly esteemed and passed on down the generations, probably accompanied by legendary tales. In *Culhwch and Olwen*, Cai (Sir Kay in later Arthurian texts) was summoned to the castle of Dyrnwch the Giant[2]. Having arrived and been taken to meet with Dyrnwch, he was requested by him to sharpen his sword, as he had heard that Cai was accomplished in this art.

At first, Cai asked him how he wished the sword blade to turn out, either dark blue or white, emphasising his skill, but Dyrnwch left the choice up to Cai to decide. Using a banded whetstone, Cai proceeded to furbish the weapon, and, as told in the tale, after he had honed it to perfection, he then

---

2 See Treasure 1.

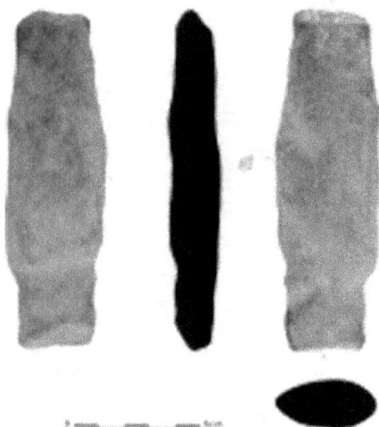

Whetstones from Roman Gaul. (ScienceDirect).

Below 19th-century image of Iron Age swords. Replica of a Celtic warrior's garments. Kelten-Keller Museum, Rodheim-Bieber, Germany. Gorinin (Wikimedia Commons).

chopped off the giant's head, which he presented to Culwrch. With Cai having achieved this for the latter, this enabled Culwrch to present it to Ysbaddaden as one of the many impossible tasks he had to perform in order to marry his daughter Olwen.

Peasant with scythe and whetstone. Jean-Pierre Norblin de la Gourdaine (1817). Bibliotheque Nationale de France. (Wikimedia Commons).

Iron swords, although appearing at around the beginning of the Iron Age in Britain and on the

Continent, did not become prevalent until around the 8th century BCE, and two types evolved. The long sword had a hilt which was often made from organic fabric, and it featured designs such as stylised anthropomorphic images. The short sword, on the other hand, possessed a hilt which was made from an alloy of copper, and which tended to have a design that was fully anthropomorphic or some kind of abstract figure. Normally, scabbards were forged from a couple of iron plates, which hung from a belt designed from iron links, although in Britain the plates at the front were sometimes made from bronze, which was not so popular on the Continent.

For centuries, the best stone in England for making whetstones was to be found at Charnwood Forest in Leicestershire, which was also used for quern stones. Nowadays, whetstones tend to be made from synthetic stone, which is of equal quality to the traditional variety; however, the natural whetstones are highly prized for the finesse of their physical appearance.

WORKS CONSULTED

Celtic Myth & Legend: An A-Z of People and Places, by Mike Dixon-Kennedy (1996).

Everyman's Dictionary of Non-Classical Mythology, compiled by Egerton Sykes (revised edition 1962).

The Mabinogion, translated by Sioned Davies (2008).

From Peneverdant: *Poems for the Land and Myths for the Old Gods of Britain* (https://lornasmithers.wordpress.com/) Wikipedia.